Black Blesse

Black, Blessed and British

Poems for reflection, performance and praise

CLAUDETTE ATHEA DOUGLAS

ISBN 978-1-8381190-0-3

A Spirit First Creatives publication from
Black Stone Press & DMC Books

Distributed By
Black Stone Press & DMC Consultancy
27 Trory Street, Norwich, UK
office@dmcconsultancy.co.uk

Remembering my sister
Carole Nathlee Douglas

Unending gratitude to all my family, friends and fellow travellers who have made my journey so far, exquisitely rewarding. Special thanks and praise to my brother Amal "Vonzo" for your tireless patience, guidance, professionalism and love.

Table of Contents

                                    continued overleaf

Foreword

It is unspeakable pleasure and pride I feel reading the manuscript of 'Black Blessed and British' written by one of my most beloved former students The Reverend Claudette Athea Douglas. The moment I began reading; the line 'Still I Rise' from Maya Angelou's poem pops into my head, as it embodies to me what Douglas has so expressively worded in her compassionate and well observed gems about her personal quest for identity, belonging and purpose.

Claudette was among the first group of students taught at the beginning of my teaching career in Jamaica, at the Dinthill Technical High School. She and her family were fresh from Britain her homeland, expressed so eloquently in the poem **Cheltenham 31039.** They were now thrust into Jamaica, the colonial motherland and immediately this fired her spirit and ignited her creative soul. She had come "home" to unearth something deep and ancestral which is delivered in the poem **Red Dirt** where she links to the aluminium soaked earth with the resistance and uprisings which shaped so much of Caribbean islands history. The poem is movingly understood in the "reddened tinge of freedoms yield".

As a student she sparked my curiosity and delight because of her maverick character and very British accent. She excelled in my English and Drama classes because of her innate creativity and a hunger to devour the culture of her new country, which was in contrast to what she was accustomed to back in England, which the poem **Go Home** lays out in the repetitive brutality of the *othering* voice.

She was such an outstanding and model student that in her senior year she was voted Head Girl for the school. After graduation and before returning to England she became a formidable actress in Jamaican theatre, both on stage and on television.

The poem *'Rio Cobre'* brings back so much personal memory. It is possibility the longest river in Jamaica. It was a river that often disrupts the lives of people living in that part of the country during the rainy season, when it would overflow its banks, make the bridge impassable, wash away people and livestock and block the roads. It flowed from the mountains in the North-Eastern part of the island down through the twists and turns of hills and gullies over the plains of St. Catherine, finally belching out into the Caribbean Sea, its final destination.

It both intrigues and inspires me, the exciting way in which Douglas uses poetry to chronicle her life's journey through the twist and turns of her struggles, being born and raised in a culture of white supremacy yet determined to discover and celebrate her own wroth . But like the "Rio Cobre River" she has finally found her purpose, her destiny by constantly re-inventing and re-imagining herself on the way, to overcome the seemingly insurmountable obstacles she encountered.

This autobiographical poetic work is colourful and powerful, both in imagery and emotion. Turning the pages of history to give glimpses of the journey of humanity itself from creation to the black people of Africa to then to colonies of the New World. The poems are indeed stories which reverberate with the immediacy, musicality and resonance of the **Talking Drums** of Africa's intersperse where the melodies of Europe, lay bare the impact and raw wounds of slavery and racial discrimination and ultimate self actualisation.

Douglas has penned a deeply uplifting collection where obstacles come to prepare us for the definitive exploration the search we all have for identify purpose and meaning which is the search that connects this work to all of us and connects us to each other.

Her work is a captivating read and well timed fresh perspective on an indelible voyage of self-discovery.

Eisenhower J. Williams (aka Stowie)

Educator (language arts & theatre; dance and acting), author, playwright, director, choreographer.
Bishop Michael Eldon School, Freeport, Bahamas

Cover of The Brownie Annual 1972

Birth

Let There Be Light

Consecrated
I am the reimbursement of eternity
Intertwining loves effortless birthing of time
Erupting from the forever fountain
Which evolves into molten gold

Everything is energy
The frequency of light
Transforming
Ageless
Purposed and powerful.

Endowed and holistic
Atoms, photons and neons integrate
Whilst, Storming, norming and free-forming
Boundless triumvirates of
hindsight, foresight and insight

Tumbling in between
the constellations of all our tomorrows
We are thrust forward
Through the windbreakers of creations
canopies

Past the majestic towers
Gem encrusted chambers
That erupt as stars
Detailed
by interstellar
friction fusion and fission
A new vision

Word sound and power
Speak us into being and
We each accept our unique mission
Where every action
Yields the gleaning of
our hidden mystery
Inscribing our history on the
living plasma of our beings

Fertilised by cosmic rays wedded to stardust
We transmute into life
Metamorphosing whilst
projected through
the divinely knitted
embryonic embrace

Concurrent curvature of eternity
We time travel in Trinity
Of the breath, water and the spirit
Radiating
Power potential and light
Propelled and moving across
the vortex of eternities
We each are individually
teleported past the oceans of subconscious
whispers
Emerging as one, yet
billions of participles vibrate into existence
beginning a road of destination

Constantly attracting the gathering of the
endless moments
That come in pristine and singular
We first appear as droplets of movement
Floating
vapours of expectation
We arise.

Osmosised and upended
Like
dew-drops
drawn back
into
the symbiosis of the universe
Daintily balanced
the maker's scales
are weighted
Each one precious
each thing an individual
every one unique
We forward to the new crossings
Juxtaposed

Our celestial heritage
intrudes like a blue print
imposed
We are the mist and the clay from carbon
and form as carbon copies of God
Those inner mysteries are already embedded
in the seat of the soul

Which shear the buds of consciousness
thinking
Beacon-like
The ignition of wonder energises
intentions when
spoken into likeness
as electricity
Gleaned from divinity
Triggers simultaneously
the lighting of never-ending stars and the
scattering of each individual planet

Passions are moulded
by the hand of genius and
Honed in the perfection of grace

Creation's evidence
Speaks for itself as
Sentinels inexorability magnetised
are drawn to follow the trail of the pilgrims
who stand immortalised
in the ever-present omens and
Landmarks along the way
Become your light

Identity

Intercultural intersectionality
conjures up a new polarity
Experienced through the washed up of
exodus shores
Pirate plunderers
face-off
Windrush wonderers
Crossing continents
rowing oars

From the ancient kingdoms of Africa's
womb
I arrive.
Prehistoric traders
architects
labourers
mercantile
vendors

uprooted embers
limitless harvest
all of whom first travelled here
when they were free

From the earliest seekers
Hardcore reapers
planters, teachers
we continue
to mould new vessels of ourselves.

Our history hinted
we would be differently tinted
by thirsty sun, and genetic perfection.

This is my situation
not a fragmentation
but a hybrid aggregation
part of everyone
that was and is.
I come.

Middle passage crossing
I also
Survived
though my past was radicalised
for I was demonised
dehumanised
colonised
yet
self-liberated
I come.

Many different views
many different clues
in shades
of skin
chants of creed
cultures collide.
We persist by way of faith.

Intercultural intersectionality
proffers a new definition
this is my recognition

expressed through the offspring of
embarkation
entwined in this space and time a newer
generation.
now migrant wonderers
stand facing
shipwrecked ponders
who are
Crossing continents again

Cheltenham 31039

Hello
Cheltenham 31039
May I help you please?
Seated on the telephone table
Proudly on display in the hallway
Excited hands lift the large red receiver
and I am answering the first call of the new
day
As now the clocks have gone forward
and daylight trumpets
its own extension
with the tick tock
which checks off
Time for vintage cider out of sight at Coxes
Meadow
Where boys laughing as they play are

hunting for newts hidden in the long
swaying grasses
Ahead the season scrumping for apples and
pears is beckoning and we
are skipping and nipping our fingers on the
long line of bursting
blackberries woven into the prickly bushes
along the hedgerow.

Hazel nuts stuffed in pockets as we
squat around or sit on mats lighting fags in
our den
Our sacred meeting space was
created by all the local kids from in our cul-
de-sac and around the neighbourhood.
it was made from collected building site
debris and anything extra we could nick
from around the boards which lead to the
grounds that wound its up of the abounded
large old Manor house that has been
standing empty for decades

Trespassing and snooping around the house
in the afternoons give us many great
adventures especially as it is rumoured to be
haunted.
Cotswold Summers holidays are action
packed always so much to do.
Our parents prioritise family time for
edutainment visits
These include jaunts to stately homes,
castles, zoos, museums and always the City
of Bath!
We must touch the seaside at Barry Island
or Western Super Mare where we collect
shells and cover Dad up to his neck in the
golden sands

When left to our own devices we are spoilt
for choice
as we can choose all day swimming at the
Lido
or the Odeon cinema watching A and B
movies

over and over again until we can anticipate
the punchlines, then onwards
window shopping up the high street, trying
on clothes in Chelsea Girl, then before we
know it we are prancing down the
Promenade
re-enacting scenes from our favourite
movies.
We play street games of British Bull Dog 123
where some battles continued on to the
evening when our parents call us in for
Supper Time.
Spontaneity and effervescent optimism are
unnoticed gifts that underpin the
foundation of our friendships and the inter-
connectedness of our lives

I am awestruck and blink with wonder on
the slopes of Daisy Bank as the hours are all
laid out before us like a ready generous plum
willing to share its inner secrets

Once our chores are finished the days are
our own
It is a scorching afternoon and we are
singing every song in Smash Hits or Disco
45 from cover to cover for hours on end until
we were hoarse from our squealing Giving
and receiving with each breath we are
overcome with the heady delirium of
fulfilment

Exhilarated and hopeful our hearts are
inspired and sprung open.
Every moment is fully experienced as all of
time is embraced.
We head to Pittville Park stopping by the
Pump Rooms then forward pursuing our
adventures, rowing on the lakes, playing
tennis then hunting for the local ghosts
under the tunnels of the large Arboretum.
We scream and run when interrupted by an
inebriated reveller who is singing loudly as

he staggers home from the Beer Festival
tents!
Throwing ourselves on the thick and springy
clover filled grass
we are convulsing with laughter and relief.

For all our regency splendour and small-
town swagger
I experience my environment as an intricate
network of hamlets, unusual spires,
and parishes woven together through
church, time, creativity and settlement
Life in widescreen Cotswold summers are
full-on and inventive
played out against the all-encompassing
canopy of countryside that punctuates the
seasons and is interwoven into emerging
perspectives

Our language of belonging to us and being
ours is knitted into the acceptance we find

in each other and all the while wildlife
teams with vibrancy and
the eye is caught by darting creatures
So my attention to detail spots individually
crafted butterflies dancing around our heads
in the breeze
Pond reeds grow upwards surrounding the
water where tadpoles are visible in spring
but now host a multitude of tiny darting
things, creatures which fly and buzz
all providing an oasis for passing birds.
Girl Guides playing hopscotch punctuate
the scene
and everything is possible as a ladybird
lands on my shoulder

Gram

Gram slam
as music gushes
from the big wooden
box as it sings...

Now you say you're lonely
You cried the long night through
Well, you can cry me a river, cry me a river
I cried a river over you

With knobs that tune in and twist out
all the way round
Turn-tabled
and transposing the global icons
so they rock and
knock socks off the silence
When sounds explode and

lots of them ignite
breaking free...

*Moon river wider than a mile I am crossing you
in style someday*

Liberated virtuosos
escape the captivity
of the hallowed frame
Where buttons some large some flat
turning always
this way and that

Vinyl pristine
black
Positioned
on the circle of life
All the while
rotating a multitude of voices
assembled with reverence and momentum...

Forever my darling our love will be true
Always and forever I'll love just only you

The illustrious past is awakened
as legends invade our space
Empowering through grace as the evidence
of their anointing is heard
They were destined to touch
this indentured soul...

Love is a many splendored thing
It's the April rose that only grows in the early
Spring

I am in awe of your multi-faceted
machinery
The magical technology that reverberates
Magnificently magnifying
Continually edifying
Fingers skilfully
touching dial
Finding the groove

the needle
exactly placed
Each disk carefully held in the centre
as the stylus holds it firm...

64-46 was my number.
Give it to me one time

Push the big switch and radio introduces a
world served up in speech and expression
unknown languages crackle into hearing
bringing remote sounding locations which
increased the space of
the living room...

Viking, North Utsire, South Utsire, Forties
Cromarty, Forth, Tyne, Dogger,
Fisher, German Bight, Humber, Thames, Dover,
Wight, Portland, Plymouth,
Biscay, Trafalgar, FitzRoy Sole, Lundy, Fastnet,
Irish Sea, Rockall, Malin, Hebrides
Bailey, Fair Isle, Faeroes, South East Iceland

Gram Slam
thank you, mam!
Selecting records was a favourite pastime for
me
Tune by tune reading the back of and inside
the cover
I uncover
the stories of the lives behind the music the
substance behind the sounds.
Fats Domino, Jonny Ace followed Nina
Simone
Brooke Benton, Syl Austin or Al Green
crooning
These tracks were played when Dad was
home...

You could hear the hoof beats pound
As they raced across the ground
And the clatter of the wheels
As they spun round and round

Gram Slam
You translated what history narrated
and replayed for posterity
what is now a legacy
Bob Marley, Elton then Queen
Top of the Pops Albums mixed with
The Sound of Philly and Northern Soul
Benny Hill or Lonnie Donegan could be
followed by
Ella Fitzgerald duetting with Louis Jordan
or was it Nat king Cole?...

I really can't stay (but baby, it's cold outside)
I've got to go away (but baby, it's cold outside)

You delivered
voices touched by God
and filled the open table of our spirits
Touching seminal signals where vibrations
which roused the dormant listener to
Remember the echo from The Ancient of
Days

encoded within our own humanity.
This gift of ingenuity
You Player of infinity
In your mechanising arms
we pivoted new stages for exploration
an incantation
Simulation of the soul
Your music made us whole
Gave us cultural girth

We were fed from birth
and elevated way beyond our own confines
Advanced through tones that set the world
alight
You brought our horizons heavenward
Culturised, harmonised and synthesised!
We were refined!

Bulky friend
There was no end
to the exploits you allowed us to create
Singing with the broom or

parties in the living room
Then a new disc would arrive brand new
from "home"...

Oh, rise Jamaica rise and let us celebrate, let's
forget the past,
independence time is here

and when the house was bursting with
family and friends
Your magic shared around nights that were
Pulsating
Liberating

You gave us autonomy our own democracy
Free to curate the soundtrack of our lives
and choose how we would define ourselves.
Booming through your speaker
When Wray and Nephew start to flow,
Babysham, Snowball and ginger wine
lubricate

all the neighbours come and dance and
celebrate...

Oh cherry, Oh Cherry, Oh baby
Don't you know I'm in love with thee?
If you don't believe its true
What have you left me to do
So long I've been waiting
For you to come right in
And now that we are together
Please make my joy run forever

Gram slam
as music gushes
from the big wooden
box as it sings
vibrates
and helps us rock

Mothers Love

Fob-watched and starched
Our mother's uniform was white and
pristine.
Shift patterns all her working life
The Nurse that is my mother nourished
ubiquitously.
As her children we were her crowning
jewels
glistening and black
We shone with olive oil and Vaseline rubbed
into our skins.
Somewhere in between breakfast, tea and
supper time
The constant routine was instilled

Eye, nose, and ear drops
a tip of Dettol in every bath

Peppered with hilarious stories of her
childhood in Jamaica where a colourful cast
of characters ignited my prolific visions.
Mother's love exposed all too many places,
fairs, circuses museums, stately homes,
theatre and cinema were just some of
voyages that were taken as a team with my
siblings

Now I see myself parenting my child
through the same route of cultural
intelligence through the lived experience
and I understand more each day the
engrained lessons and unbreakable bond
planted by mother's dedication and duty

I remember every spoonful of malt and cod
liver oil, finding a warm toasty hot water
bottle that seemed to miraculously appear
under the eiderdown just before bedtime

She carefully crafted our growing
around a creative circle of
laughter, love and strict enforcement of daily
chores which
we had to execute with absolute precision

Mother's standards were high
dust would not be tolerated!
Skirting boards were spotless the house was
always to be spick and span from head to
foot
Nestled round our kitchen table
childhood home felt strong and stable
dinners were eaten there in the evenings
and Monopoly and Frustration played out
boisterously into the night
if it was a weekend
or it was bedtime at 7.30pm
Up in our bedrooms we're free to chill out
and pursue our paths

Mother's ground rules nurtured our ability
gardened our imagination and forged a
capacity to be humane
Our mates would often invite themselves
to tea hoping for a full Jamaican supper after
school
They knew my mother ruled the roost but
they would always be welcomed.
Our basement became a go to hub
that resembled the united nations gathering
space
Barnardo's kids, hippies' gypsies and most of
the eclectic types who loved to listen to
Motown, jazz and reggae music on Friday
nights
Bodies would crowd into our downstairs
sanctuary that Dad had built for us.
Mother's love propagated, reproved
disciplined and guided us as we grew,
shaped by her pruning

Undaunted she brought many so many
elements together through an emotionally
sensitive capacity and force of personality
Mother's love has bequeathed a bloom
whereby life has blossomed into a
comprehensive facility
to love others without prejudice
unconditionally

She was a child of Empire
One of many who came here to help rebuild
this country after the 2nd World War.
She recounted the incidences, the insults
she had endured yet remained proud of her
sacrifice
Proud of what she had been able to
contribute.
She told us tales of the indignities she had
faced, of ugly words, spits and racist insults
that amazingly did not crush her or change
her to bitterness.
I find this remarkable

Though these experiences had hurt her she
was always willing to understand and
explain the ignorance and fear that hide
behind hatred

Her life's response is to carry on living with
characteristic magnanimity and aplomb
I have evolved, taught by her example
and so, I celebrate the generosity of this
inheritance
to genuinely live without hate.

Go Home

Go home!
Nignog, Sambo[1], Coon[2].
Black Bitch, Rubber lips
You African Baboon

Piss off!
Monkey
Jungle bunny, wog[3]
We don't want your sort round here
Sling your hook, black dog

---

[1] Antiquated term used to describe a person of mixed European and Amerindian and African ancestry.

[2] Shortening of *Raccoon*, first used as a racial slur in 1745.

[3] Used to describe an individual of Indian descent, an acronym for *Westernised Oriental Gentlemen,* From *Golliwog*, a dark-skinned doll and also a term used to describe any dark-skinned individual.

Sod off!
Nigger[4] baby, ape features
Bitch.
We don't play with blackies
You Biafran[5] witch.

Get stuffed!
Blackie
Why don't you, go back home
Black bitch, rubber lips
You African baboon.

---

[4] From French *nègre* and Portuguese *negro*- a black person.
Is regarded one of the most offensive words in the English
Language.

[5] From Biafra a former West African State that is part of
modern Nigeria, to be extremely malnourished.

Fight Club Rap

Metaphors of love for my father

I am a survivor
a mystical striker
Learned to box aged ten
when daddy showed
me how
He put me on the ropes
then
he taught me to
weave and duck
and he taught me how to move and bow

Studied how to take it on the chin
Then to dance upon my toes
Learned how to jab and swing
Then aim right for the nose

I am the hot-stepper
lyrical master
Like Ali in the ring
Come with alms-house in my space
Like chuck Berry's Ding- a- ling
I will rearrange your face!
Yeah so!
Trials have often laid me low
When life has been offensive
so
I respond with the killer blow
because
I know how to box defensive

I just will not stay beat
Get me
the stamina queen
I will get back on my feet
the greatest comeback ever seen

My personal revolution will be scrutinised
hypostasised and digitised

It is the truth that is so revealing
It is the progress that comes out of healing.

The profiles in The Boxing News and the
photos in The Ring
Revealed improvised lives of former champs
and taught me many things
like
Every great warrior must learn from defeat,
Sonny Liston, Joe Dempsey George Forman
and all
but the greatest lessons are not learned on
your feet
but after you've experienced your greatest
falls

You see
life cannot be all KOs or beating the
opposition
it includes being able to rotate in your
corner
and understanding how you re-position.

Endurance develops so you know how to
improve
Patience grows so you find your own groove

So what!
Well when I got knocked down or out
I had to learn how to self- motivate
How to face up to my own depression
Dismantle my own self-hate

Pull myself out of my dejection.
Reject my own self-loathing
Resolve my inner schisms
Reactivate my own soul
Reevaluate my own mission.

Legend
I know now how to fuel my spirit
to nurture me and replenish my mind
and resuscitate my consciousness
and reflect on what I find

Yeah so!
I am still dancing on my toes
I am still thinking on my feet
I'm still breathing through my nose
whilst drumming my own beat

When my back is against the wall
I will come out swinging
When all hell is breaking loose
I now come out singing
When my show hits the ropes
I will find new phrase's
I jab with my expression
I counter punch you with my all my praises

I developed my left hook
and perfected my own swing
I move classy like Sara Vaughn voicing
That's where I learned to dip and bop
I am the crusader of Worship-rejoicing
Spirituals jazz reggae and hip hop

Through re-evaluating from my own story
I am now able to actualise
My personal USP resonates
I know how to survive

Umbilically anchored histories
Understanding when to dodge or weave
Unearthing who I was born to be
The purpose I come to achieve

I have learned
How to turn my mind to any thing
To reconstruct, regenerate and re-conceive
In the face of loss and doubt
to continue to believe

So what?
I now throw punches with my songs and
plays
Strike my blows with creativity
Beat the crap out of my inertia
and free the best of me.

I am a survivor
A mystical striker
Learned to box from I was ten
'Cause my daddy showed me how.

Face Off

You have been identified!
I know who you are now
Back off!
You multitude of vipers
Begone! Ignorance
Retreat! Hatred
Depart! Racism
Withdraw! Xenophobia
Flee! Fear
Go! Intolerance
Go! Rejection
Go! Homophobia
Go! Hostility
Go! Cruelty
Go! Blame
Go! Poverty
Go! Subduction
Go! Starvation

Go! Shame
Go! Miseducation
Go! Greed
Go! Enmity
Go! Inequality
Go! Injustice
Go! poverty
Go! Enslavement
Vamoose! You vexed and embittered snare
Go! Enemy of life
Begone!
You foul and wicked spirit
Cast yourself out
Turn yourself off
Be ye extinguished
forever.
Leave this earth and find some other planet
to plague!

Paraffin Solider

Tall and black or green
Iron clad armour embellished
Our valiant knight who heroically fended off
shrill shards of cold Cheltenham mornings

Silent and stoic the overlooked giant
stood to attention
and wherever he was needed
he moved

His honour integrity and warmth
surrounded our growing with love.
Steady and unchanging we gathered around
his feet to roast nuts in his grate
light cigarettes through his nose
heat curling irons on his crown

and chatted whilst we exchanged the
highlights of our day

The unseen guest at very meal and muted
witness to every midnight feast
He was the onlooker to every
communication He became the stalwart
enforcer
shielding us from the vicissitudes of the
seasons
Unnoticed he watched us play and heard our
crying too
We fed him Esso Blue!

This purple elixir was guzzled down greedily
while the condensation streamed down our
rattling window panes
as our eyes stung and reddened with his
fumes

Get too close and your veins turned blue
stay too far and you missed his wholesome
embrace
He took centre stage in our basement
Eavesdropping on every conversations
He was a perpetual in my formative years
and his heavily hooded eyes flickered
approvingly with flecks of fire
warming our desire and fuelling our
youthful dreams

He made our waking bearable
Coming in from the cold
he welcomed us home every day
My paraffin solider
Standard Bearer
You were cheerleader and supporter
even through memory shedding light and
warmth

English Spring

Daisy and buttercup scatter o'er the field
in yellow-white confusion
dancing with joy my heart does yield
to English spring colour profusion

Summer spills over irrepressible with
splendour
butterflies and ladybirds come into their
own
drenched in the sunlight I sit and I ponder
and listen to the sound of hoof on stone

Autumn's appearance a promenade of
contrasts
Bronzed leaves and conkers drop all around
nature announces her kaleidoscopic

broadcast
Rag and bone pony cart offers the sound

Winter sneaks up with her nippy embrace
Salvation Army band play in our cul-de-sac
after church
Cowslips, snowdrops and red berries
cover all space
the perfume of the pine wood,
heather and birch

Ahh! here spring comes again, completely
reborn
with the refrain of the dawn chorus new
Fragrance the scent of the newly mowed
lawn
Silent the sunshine and morning dew

Daisy and buttercup scatter o're the field
in yellow-white confusion
dancing with joy my heart does yield
to English spring colour profusion

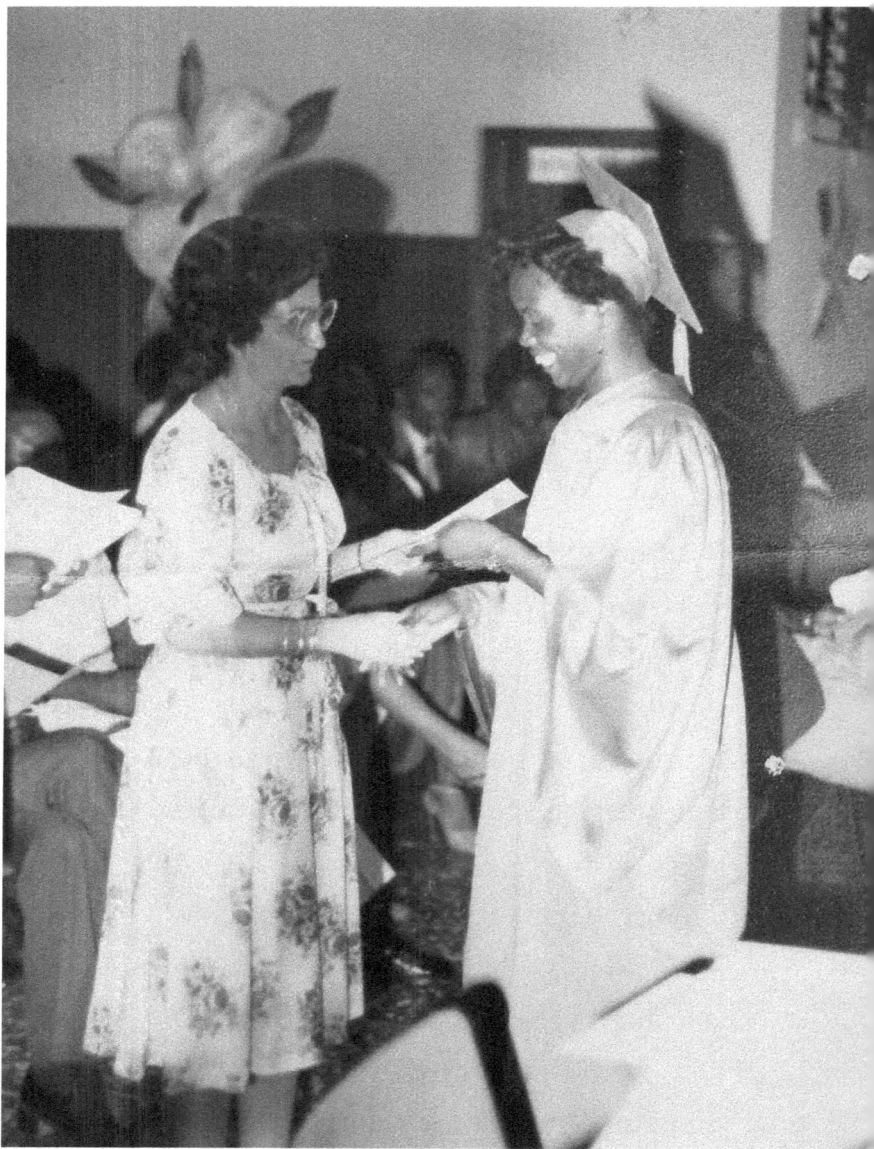

Graduation from Dinthill Technical High School

Belonging

Red Dirt

Bitter-sweet Bauxite brimming
over with
enflamed minerals
that spread
bejewelled droplets of
embedded richness
hidden by the
forgotten past.

Golden bronzed pathways
continue onwards
Gushing out
mirage-like shimmers of rosy dusts
stretching far into the
heat soaked horizon
pulverised by a thousand
pilgrims that walked these
planes when
Cudjoe led the Mormons
and the wealth of the ground
was understood in
the reddened tinge of Freedoms yield.

Sweet Bamboo

I saw them from a place
their swaying lengths extend towards me.
Beneath the ledge where I had perched
Sugar cane beckons and billows
majestically

For furlongs, more than I could stare
these sun soaked haughty reeds refused to
bow
but in their proud resilient glare
I found my history
anyhow

On plantation, slopes, hills or plain
their presence here transmits my past.
Stubborn backs withstanding pain
transported, replanted,

still holding
fast

Whenever in need of refreshment
their juicy flesh replenish me,
and within the harvest of her breast
I suckle nectar
fervently

Whenever I am lost or down
their noble reeds entreat me still
to likewise, find within a crown
whose is rooted to the earth
flourishing at will.

Morning Glory

Elohim
I rise up early
in your name

El Shadi
I wake with your
kiss on my brow
the flame of your
love
has shielded
my sleep
and I have
been rewarded with another piece of
heaven

Moments to
become your canvas

An image
enlightened
Imprinted in the
whispered mist
that seeps through

the dappled haze of morning
embossed and refracted in rainbows shard
that glint in humbled recognition of Glory
saluted by the trees that stand in the garden

El Elyon
This day is freshly made and mine
eyes are widely open
I am delighted by you
I lift up my heart
towards you

My soul is outstretched
for the first, breaths of morning
and I am
uplifted once again

by the endless
possibilities
of another new day

Rio Cobre

Snake river
round Bog-Walk way
you have wrapped
yourself around the
mountains
of the central plains

Old continental
you boast hidden knowledge
of many histories
Of dug out boats
invading troops
runaway
slaves and buried
treasure troves

Haunted silhouettes
as the Golden Table
dips and fall back
into the past legends
round the gully bend

Each corner
hides rapid waters and
buried Moorish Jars
Awe inspiring
your deep calls to the deeper
endless search
we have within

Mirrored image
of a nation
continually
in the grip
of its own discovery.
Spanish worm
you curl your history and snare

those dat nuh know River Road
and Flat Bridge corner.

When rain come hard
you buss di bank side and all must look as
the
heart at the centre
is flooded
cleansed
then restored
and then yuh let us through only when yuh
ready.
Then we march across
crisscrossing yet still so much
in awe of you.

Black Peoples Sunday

Mamas moaning
groaners so holy
souls that thirst
for the quenching
knowledge of
God's grace

Burdens lifted
sin aborted
amid the large brimmed hats
ample arms
and curious customs
carried through
millennium
on talking drums and echoed rhythms
chants and songs

Children whisper
pastors blister
with the heat of fire of the spoken word.
The place where
Christ is heard
Loads are shifted
hearts uplifted
as screams of redemption
fill the rafters where rat-bats' hang
and the air is punctuated with shouts of
Hallelujah! Hallelujah!

Hey Madman

People called him Hombré
Children would scorn his nakedness
and old ladies would look away
from the flying genitalia
that flapped themselves
ludicrously around
his grey dirt-caked limbs.
His hair
was matted like a mighty oak
standing over two feet tall atop his massive
frame
Strong arms, firm features.
His eyes
haunting hazel slits that
seemed to stare past your soul
looking outwards toward the Jamaican
sunrise.

Hombré would earnestly and methodically
gather mango skins,
bottle tops and banana trash
from the overflowing stinking gutters
around the markets iron gates

Preoccupied with his task
Hombré was moved by a compulsion to
work
as he was always in urgent pursuit
of his own fulfilment
He progressed with purpose
busy with the moments of his day
"Hey mad man"
"Hey mad bwoy"
"Ah weh you really come from?"

Little children would sometimes follow him
through the streets
Sheepishly staring at his massive
endowments

"How you so dirty and stink
and tan so bad?"
"How you toe nail dem so long?".
They giggled childishly and squealed as
naughty children do
before running off
and leaving him alone once again
with his thoughts.

Paradoxically
many people fed him
Unkindly
some people mocked him
Unfairly
a few people feared him
Unconsciously
other people ignored him
Yet, Instinctively
most people felt compassion
and were moved by the very sight of him

Captivating vision
this quintessential afraid giant
who circumvented central Spanish Town
like a living colossus
Impoverished now by the enclosed and
mysterious captivity of his own thinking
His was now a mind now firmly closed off to
everyone but himself
Was this his choice, his armour or
protection?
Or a traumatic response to loss and pain,
or perhaps the despair of a bitter rejection?

His silhouette cast a large shadow in front of
the old Court House building
where the dipping sun set him apart
like a bronzed behemoth.
For a people not yet free of the memory
of the slavers whip
and still yoked to the
infringements of colonialism

Hombré echoed a stark reminder of a
brutally enforced status anxiety
where a lower rung on the precarious
tropical social ladder
could await the vulnerable, lost or insane
No safety net here to catch you when you
fall.
"Him go and come"
This was the colloquially given explanation
for Hombrés plight

Here sound mind and madness are
understood to be either side of the same
coin
as interchangeable as circumstance and
fortune
understandable as the old wisdoms
that moved down the generations
through word of mouth and lived
experiences where the residue of hurt still
resides.

Some passers-by would throw him small
change
from their pockets
as others would hail him from moving
vehicles as they passed him on the road.
"Big up Hombré, ah wha gwan big man?"
Market vendors and onlookers nodded
knowingly when he appeared on his rounds
all sure they knew Hombré's story

His Parish was Spanish Town.
His regular patch began near the market
leading its path to the old Record Office
that blossomed out into the still impressive
imperial square.
Here large gun cannons and memorials to
European invaders hint at the turmoil of a
multitude of past majestic aspirations
where the splendour had long since been
replaced by decay

Nobody really knew where he had come
from.
They say he had appeared in the market over
two decades ago in his naked state
with a copy of The Bible
and The Voyages of Homer
wrapped in a hessian cloth bag
He did not seem to know who he was or
perhaps he had chosen to forget

This was where the legend of Hombré
began.
He would circle his way in between the
everyday dramas of
his loud and colourful congregation
Amid the guinep strewn baskets, the shouts
from the hilarious street hawkers where
fruit sellers with soursops and hampers
laden with star apples, limes and imported
shoes from Cayman Island.
Dennis Brown was booming from a sound
system in Miss Gees Rum Bar

while Hand cart boys and Sky-Juice sellers
navigated their way around the large
potholed roads
and the streets were full of life and a
vibrancy that fuelled its own energy.

Gossip hushed and oft repeated would
invariably follow Hombré's pathway as the
stories of his "past" were told with
creativity, pathos, vulgarity and humour

Some voices said he was a victim of
deportation from Mandeville where it was
rumoured that council workers rounded up
their mentally ill and dispatched them,
by night
into unsuspecting Parishes!
Others would be saying that he had come
from great wealth and somehow lost it all on
the horses at Caymanas Park
or to another form of addiction
Other voices said that he had been betrayed

by a lover
who broke his heart and mind
when he had caught her with his best friend
There were so many version of Hombré's
past including the one that said, Hombré
was the illegitimate son
of a former Prime Minster
Yet I had been told many times for certain
that he had been a Rhodes scholar of
international renown
but too much study had institutionalised
his thinking
and the pressure of other people's
expectations had reduced him to a tortured
existence.
Are we ever truly known to anyone but
ourselves?

Hombré was a Jamaican enigma
he came without a past and previous identity
yet people had created new ones for him

Everybody ultimately belongs to the
collective.
"Even if yuh nuh born yah, yuh still deh on
yah".

I never once saw him beg or ever once heard
him curse
His hulk-like nakedness would promenade
heroically along Martin Street with the
blazing afternoon sun casting shadows
that played with my fertile teenage
imagination.
I had not expected to be confronted
With the audacious stark complexity
of my own history.
My British sensibilities were being refined
by "out of many one people" and the
Caribbean generosity in which we allow
each other's
to coexist
without being medicated,
restrained or incarcerated.

Incongruous
I felt strangely connected to his soul and
somehow in awe of his dignified travail
He resembled a latter-day warrior or
Prophet waving an old tree branch in his
hand.
Moses-like
He was muttering and singing,
battling his own demons
as he picked up a still smoking cigarette
from the curb
He drew a large intake and then began to
gather more banana trash
warring with his past
whilst daily defining his own future.

"Hey Mad man,
mad boy,
put on some clothes nuh"

Free Paper Bun

End of term[6]

End of term and we fly out the classrooms
with the reckless abandonment of summer.
June plums nice and ripe
bulge in our pockets.
Uniforms
ironed and pristine
against clear blue Caribbean skies
and we rush along
to sneak down to the citrus groves
behind the cow pen
where we fill our guts
with orange vintage.
Khakied boys tease

---

[6] Is a Jamaican saying that makes reference to slaves
documents of freedom. When the documents are burned, the
slave must return to work. It is now commonly used in
reference to school holidays coming to an end

and we shriek with
joy and hype.
Lips are glossed
and every baby hair is in place.
We were
pubescent pouting perfection.
Studious and hopeful in the
confines of our esteemed institution
The holidays beckon and
our bodies are changing
as we recognise
that we cannot stay young forever.

Hastily we grab each moment
in each other's dreams,
country children, townies, and foreigners
we all have visions
of a world we seek to
stand astride
of a freedom we
dream of and believe
will be attainable

as our own enfranchisement

is yet to come.

Still

free paper bun

Froggy B

For my Headmaster

"And who is the student?
One who studies of course
You don't come here to box young lady
This English report card says all you have
done is fight
Well let me tell you why you are here
You come to pick up the book and the pen
to exercise your intellect
discover your capacity
and nurture your inner talents
develop your own perspectives
but most importantly
grow tenacity, informed opinions
and make something good of yourself!"

Factor Non Verba
Deeds Not Words

You opened the minds
for all of us searchers

Polymathic
National
Celebrated educator
You encouraged all of us dreamers
Head teacher
Waymaker
Headmaster

You built the stage for all of us performers
Visionary
Head man
Versatile
Social icon
You levelled the field for all of us runners
Manager
Mystic
Messenger
You programmed spiritual advancement into
all of your students.

Blood Fire

Bloodfire!
di cos' ah living higher
and mi daughter Sue deh breed
She can't get nuh job, and she start fi rob
and now she can't stop smoke up di weed

Bloodfire!
the devil is a liar
and life is a bitch when she ready
the system is bent
all the money is spent
and di taxes dem just getting more and more
heavy

Bloodfire!

dem tief [6] mi car tyre!

Then ah so man ah turn inna dog?

Good people are turning bad

and the bad dem ah tun inna hog!

Bloodfire!

expression still diyah

---

[6] Jamaican patois, thief.

FIRM SPORTS & LEISURE
in association with THE VOICE Newspaper
in response to unparalleled demands
PRESENT THE RETURN OF THE ORIGINAL

BUP$

OPENS 3rd AUGUST - 27th AUGUST at
The New Dick Sheppard Theatre,
Dick Sheppard School, Tulse Hill, SW2

NO DIBBI DIBBIES

NOT FOR
WEAK HEARTS!

CENSORED

"Weh BUP$ Deh!?!

"Excellent . . . not
to be missed"
South London Guardian

"Recommend it to
your friends . . ."
Caribbean Times

"Outrageous . . ."
The Guardian

"Highly
recommended"
Time Out

Fast moving . . .
thrilling . . .
exciting"
The VOICE

**NOMINATED FOR THE
NATIONAL FRINGE
THEATRE AWARDS**

sponsored by
FIRM SPORTS & LEISURE

DICK SHEPPARD
YOUTH CENTRE

96

Becoming

When Fathers Die and Leave You

When fathers die and leave you
everything freezes in the moments you no
longer have him here on earth
and the dreams you never fulfilled
in his presence
have crystalised in obscure obstacles
that crack in the bleeding throat of loss
When fathers die and leave you
hope evaporates and are trampled
where pain converges into unknown depths
that life mercifully had previously
kept hidden.

Caverns of feelings
lie engulfed in despair and anger emerges
like a ferocious friend

that must have more pity if it is to be
understood and placated

Shards of something deep and hurtful
like regret for
things which cannot be healed
except by grace and time.
Old wounds that need repair
Old tears that need drying
and aloneness that never leaves the place
where daddy lived.

Remorseful

Sitting at the dimly lit table
the gathering dusk is piqued
and speaks
of a day not fully attempted.
The coffee stands cold
and half drunk in the cup
that stares back to cosset each flowing tear
springing from a space allocated to
the language that only God understands.

So today I keep on crying
in snot running
shoulder hunching
stomach churning
convulsions that contort the face
and shake the very foundations of my soul.
Falling watery sobs

for all the wasted
efforts in the frail
frivolities of fruitless
pursuits
Sobs for actions without principles
Cries for decisions without wisdom
Time wasted on
a world full of doubts
and anxieties without foundation.

I sobbed as my face has grown older
My responses more blurred
My steps more uncertain.
Time has come to be my tormentor
and my friend
A rippled yarn of
competing moods
Warfare with contending perspectives
Now tears are to grow my gratitude
for every opportunity
Even those squandered in ignorance

I cry whilst grasping the lessons
my conscience is teaching me
from an inner place
that is sore and taut
yet reassuringly welcoming and familiar
I cry because life has been
the supreme teacher and master
and I at times
the tardy arrogant. reluctant pupil
who must now find the discipline
to learn with dulled reflexes
and worn sensibilities

Tears are a language that God understands
as the salty liquid
stings the rims of my eyes.
I see my reflection
In the panes of the window
and reddened sockets a
and a puffy face stares back

Although I am frayed at the edges
something has broken and freed me up from
the inside.
I am somewhere being remade
a recycled raiment...
I am resolved again.

Standing up I move slowly to the sink
turn on the cold tap
bend, and soak my face then hold it
reverently in my hands.
I realise I have been bending there for hours
and water has soothed me and has soaked
through to my blouse.
The evening has come and the clouds are
grey black as they steel across
the vast expanse of sky
Suddenly I take a deep inward breath
and instantly feel connected to the first
twinkly star of evening
An omen perhaps or a metaphor of hope
I stretch fully upwards and move.

All the pain of yesterday
has vanished from my right shoulder!
I still have time to express my heart to the
world
Gathered up by compassion
anchored to the Universe where my
vulnerability serve my emerging humanity

Encouraged
Irritated
Inspired
Challenged
Exhilarated
Repositioned and logged onto the nook
where I am found
I move inwards and upwards magnetised to
the trajectory of my spirit.
Enhanced
Cleansed
Honest and humbled
I am yet strangely determined
to work well with mystery

weave the majesty
and welcome whatever it is
I have left to discover
of myself!

In All Things

I will see God in all things
For in everything that remains
God is part of that existence
I will look with gladness
at the mountains and streams
and be placated by the crusade of the clouds
intersecting as seamless white turrets of sky
I will be elevated by the
tranquillity of the winds
that come as ushers
whispering their strange tune
to remind my soul to pray

I will see God in all life
and acknowledge him
through the serenity of slumber
and even in death

as we circumvent the gates of hell
bound for everlasting glory.
Holy, is everything that is
as we become part of
the great mystery of this unity

I will see God in all things
and be awestruck
by the splendour of the kingdom of nature
being reconciled through the harmony
of the energy of life
All I have been given
will constantly bring me to my feet
as I stand in praise of life,
this gift from Glory

When my womb stretched
to hold my child
I saw His honour adorn my life
When His angels summoned my father
and sister home
I beheld the flawless

fleeting prize
we hold in those we love

I will see God in all things,
for when despair is answered by joy
and challenges are found solutions
my heart is fortified.
Holy God of Zion
because of your transforming
unction to function
I see You in everything.

Royal Sunset

Sparkling orange blessed skies
give way to evensong.
Natures' chants
inexorably sound
the end of another day
as the sun is wrapped
in her blanket of night time
Warm and large
the enveloping darkness
stretches outward
across Brockwell Park.

Snails move across the path
in a bid for safety and cover of leaves
the duck pond is quiet
as the birds are resting

and the last of the people are heading home.
Languid and transformational
the unexpected warmth and sunshine
had held the day which now
draws itself to a close.

Lovers find hope
Children retrieve their dreams
as a swarm of Green Parakeets
populate the large fern tree
at the edge of the paddling pool.

This Life

I want to treasure
hold and weave it
I must find pleasure
and completely retrieve it.
I wish to stock take
and renovate it
I must now re-imagine
and re-calibrate it.

I seek to measure mix
and knead it
prove it, and let it rise.
I have to care for
share and explore it
Fashion, tap dance
and pursue it

It's so precious
I don't want to lose it
it's the only one I got
this life

So if I wake up and find that I missed it
that I messed up
or mucked up
or missed it
I can never rewind or re- run it
It's the only one I've got
this life

I am going to walk it
Even if I have to tight-rope it
I will take that deep breath
And step to it
At least I can that I troubled it
It's the only one I got
this life

Woman Transformer

For my daughter

Woman Transformer
Gleaning from the yield
Herbs incubator
Mineral ground breaker
Sewing seed in fields

Woman Transformer
Weaving cloth from yarn
Bearing fruit
Making bread
Nation feeder
Love generator
Moulding clay in palm

Woman Transformer
Communing with her soul

Creating nests, collecting bits,
Makings of a home
Artisans', travellers, fortune hunters,
teachers
Merchants, workers, big dream reachers
Building cities from wood and stone

Woman Transformer
Queen of her own domain
Enduring
Persistent
Steadfast
Resistant
For all the wave makers
Pioneers, earth shakers

Unconventional originals
Priceless, irrepressible
Breathless risk takers
Leaders, Freedom makers
Learning, Pruning.
Cultivating, Brewing

Woman Transformer
Warrior and prophetess
Strategic thinker
History linker
Shaping destiny
Making history
Female agency expressed

Praise Songs

I am No Longer Inspired by Hatred

Healing

I am no longer inspired by hatred anymore
You know I am free from human bondage
I will not be inspired by pain anymore
I am free from human bondage

I am coming into purpose
I am coming into focus
I got to name it, got to tame it
Got to claim my destiny
I will not be encumbered by the debris of my
past life
I hold it and restore it with love and alchemy

I am no longer inspired by hatred anymore
You know I am free from human bondage

I will not be inspired by pain anymore
I am free from human bondage

I am coming into glory
I am walking into progress
Got to mould it, got to sculpt it
I will illustrate my own story.
I will not be persuaded that my life has no
meaning
I will use it, through time, to reach infinity

I am no longer inspired by hatred anymore
You know I am free from human bondage
I will not be inspired by pain anymore
I am free from human bondage

I am climbing Jacobs Ladder
and I am seeing all things holy
I am propelled in height
above all that I see
In the valley of awareness
Under the shadow of his glory

El-Shaddai increases into eternity.

I am no longer inspired by hatred anymore
You know I am free from human bondage
I will not be inspired by pain anymore
I am free from human bondage

I am a Warrior

Transformation

I am a warrior
I am a warrior out of Africa
Queen Nzinga I am Yaa Asantewaa
I am a Natty, out of Egypt
I am
Out of Nanny's line
I am an old time Dreadlocks

As the Lion sleeps
Who will rouse I up?
For I am Judah, and the sceptre shall not
depart my hand
Said I am on a pilgrimage I have Jah to
praise
So if you're not happy Dread,
then gwan yuh ways

I am a warrior, Out of Africa
Queen of Sheba I am Cleopatra
I am natty, out of Nubia, I
I am out of Nanny's line
An old time Dreadlocks

This is a pilgrimage
I have I road to trod,
so if you see I dread, then wish I well.
Cause I'm a centurion I have Jah works to do
So, if you still live the lie
You can't be true

I am a warrior, Out of Africa
Queen of Sheba I am Cleopatra
I am natty, out of creation,
I is from foundation
I'm an old time Dreadlocks

I Pray

Faith

I pray, You know I pray
Teach me Jah Jah what I must say

I pray and I pray and I pray Jehovah Jireh
I pray and I pray He quench I thirst
I slip at the stream of life and I am Irie
I pray and I am trodding, ever spirit first

For when we stop and see the earth
in all her glory
All of life as a precious flow of divinity
We will dethrone our oppressor
and remove our tyrants and celebrate a
world that's trading fair and free

I pray, you know I pray
Teach me Jah Jah what I must say

I pray and I pray and I pray Jehovah Jireh
I pray and I pray he quench I thirst
I slip at the stream of life and I am Irie
I pray and I am trodding, ever spirit first

I pray that the right of the girl is equal to
her brother,
and we can reap from bounty that is ours for
free
And if we free up the mill from mountains
and the gain from silos
we can feed those who and starve to death in
poverty

I pray, You know I pray
Teach me Jah Jah what I must say

I pray and I pray and I pray Jehovah Jireh
I pray and I pray He quench I thirst
I slip at the stream of life and I am Irie
I pray and I am trodding, ever spirit first

I pray we make away for a brand-new
harvest
so the dolphin and whale can return to the
sea.
And weapons of hate and war are replaced
by reasoning,
for peace cannot be hostage to brutally

I pray. You know I pray
Teach me Jah Jah what I must say

I pray and I pray and I pray Jehovah Jireh
I pray and I pray He quench I thirst
I slip at the stream of life and I am Irie
I pray and I am trodding, ever spirit first

Redemption Story

Fulfilment

Adam came to prove the law
Hallelujah
Abraham found what faith is for
Hallelujah
Noah came to build the ark
Hallelujah
so we would live to play our part
Hallelujah

Who will come and sing with me
Hallelujah
where love creates our harmony
Hallelujah
Who will come and build with me
Hallelujah

a world that's free from enmity
Hallelujah

Moses came to lead the way
Hallelujah
for a better hope and brighter day
Hallelujah.
Joseph came to stop the drought
Hallelujah
God took us in and he will lead us out
Hallelujah

Who will come and sing with me
Hallelujah
where love creates our harmony
Hallelujah
Who will come and build with me
Hallelujah
a world that's free from enmity
Hallelujah

David came to win the war
Hallelujah
Solomon learned what peace is for
Hallelujah

Who will come and sing with me
Hallelujah
where love creates our harmony
Hallelujah
Who will come and build with me
Hallelujah
a world that's free from enmity
Hallelujah

Diaspora Uprise

For my sister Carole

I will rise again
like the Phoenix from the fire
I am up on high again

I found my wings and flying higher
I will rise again
Like the Phoenix through the flames
I can fly again
I have found my path, I am on my way

I have been down I've been out
I have been hurt, and been I have been used
and I've been broken
I took a fall and was out for the count
I've lost my way I was self-abused
I left words I should have said unspoken
but I when found the light inside of me

that seeped through from the cracks within
my soul
I knew that my spirit was
reviving me
reminding me

The power of love is what makes you whole
I will rise again
like the Phoenix from the fire
I am up on high again
I found my wings and flying higher
I will rise again

Like the Phoenix through the flames
I can fly again
I have found my path, I am on my way

Well I have been lame I've been broke
I've been wayward and completely lost
control of my life
I have been anxious I've been depressed

I have been frightened and oppressed
I was in darkness

But the fire within us
can reignite,
regenerate,
rejuvenate,
recommit
and reconnect you
with the purpose of our life

That's why I will rise again
like the Phoenix from the fire
I am up on high again
I found my wings and flying higher
I will rise again
Like the Phoenix through the flames
I can fly again
I have found my path, I am on my way

Talking Drums

Continuity

We came to this land as full vessels
not brought here empty
but full of knowledge culture and faith
We have sung of our ancestors
and have cried for our forefathers

We mourned for our customs
and have hoped for a distant land
Yet we continue to walk with our past
which nourishes and speaks to us from the
place where God lives
and it is from here that our
new possibilities and realities are created.

Milton Keynes UK
Ingram Content Group UK Ltd.
UKHW020854180224
438010UK00013B/190